Scaling to 7 Figures
Kasie T. Smith

Copyright

Copyright © 2024 by Kasie T. Smith.
All rights reserved.
In no way is it legal to reproduce, duplicate, or transmit any part of this document in either electronic means or in printed format.
Recording of this publication is strictly prohibited and any storage of this document is not allowed unless with written permission from the publisher.

Preface

I grew up in poverty. At one point, I lived in a house that had such bad roof damage that there were holes in the roof... and holes rotted through the floor right below. I have eaten food that my family dug out of grocery store dumpsters, had the lights cut off, had the electricity cut off, and all of the other things that come along with growing up poor. Our family of 7 slept in one room, so we could all have heat. We got our clothes at yard sales and often had tattered clothes and shoes, covered in stains and holes.

I am not saying this to start out some sad story. I am saying this because I want you to see that anyone can create change in their lives. If you come from less, you may just have to work harder than those who have the resources more readily available to them.

In today's economy, I find myself struggling to see the world with balance at times. There is a HUGE part of me that always believes, "God will provide." There is also a big part of me that always comes out from behind and says, "But don't be foolish and take Him for granted. Work hard. Fight for what you want. Stay humble"

I am writing this book for my believers, my pushers. You know that there is a better life out there for you, and you are going to go grab it.

Everyone does not share the same mentality or perspectives. I know this. I am not here to change anyone's belief systems. I am here to help those who already share the belief that all things are possible with faith and hard work.

When I started my business, I knew that I could make something of it. I pulled out no money for the first 3 years, because my husband and I were already 6 figure earners. I wanted to keep everything in the business and continue to invest in the company's growth. Not all of my investments were wise ones though. In fact, I spent some money very poorly. Here are some of the examples of mistakes I made:

1. In late 2022, I paid a company $55k to start and manage an Amazon store for me. I bought more than $60k worth of inventory for the store, and then (due to an improper account transfer) our Amazon store was stolen from us with no way to recover it.
2. In mid 2023, I paid $10k for an online training that taught me how to create online courses. It was so horrible. All of the modules were focused around mindset and how to be successful, and it hardly focused on course creation at all! My Audible account is filled with mindset books, and I am the most positive person that my husband believes he has ever met! Oh, this was a sad waste of $10k, with no refunds.
3. In early 2023, I paid $10k for an online training to teach you how to start an Amazon store. The training company went bankrupt and closed, and I even found out that Amazon offered almost all of this training for free in their seller portal. That was a heartbreaker.

Despite these mistakes, my SIDE BUSINESS still brought in more than $965k in 2023. By the end of June in 2024, we have already earned over $725k this year. I told my family that this was going to be our first 7 figure year, and I honestly don't think they believed me when I said it. They often make comment to me about how they think I'm crazy or how I work too much and need to just slow things down and take a break.

So, what point am I trying to make here? Your mind controls how you see the world. Your mind controls whether you see my story as a success story or a story filled with failures. Your mind allows you to see the world as being filled with opportunity or filled with hopelessness.

If you believe taking a risk will lead to a reward, you are probably more of a glass half full type of person. My glass is not half full. It is full. I want you to feel that yours is too, so I have compiled a list of life tips that I have used to guide me to a place where I feel that I have success in my career, relationships, and health. Best wishes, and I hope that you find great success that aligns with your values and beliefs.

Disclaimer

This book has been written for information/advice purposes only. Every effort has been made to make this book as complete and accurate as possible, from the perspective of the writer. However, there may be mistakes in typography or content and the author and publisher shall not be responsible for any errors or omissions. The author and publisher do not warrant or represent at any time that the contents within are guaranteed to be accurate, as they are solely considered to be advice based and due to the rapidly changing nature of the world. This book is meant to be used as a guide, not as the ultimate source of information.

The author and publisher shall have neither liability nor responsibility to any person or entity with respect to any loss or damage caused or alleged to be caused directly or indirectly by this book. In practical advice books, like anything else in life, there are no guarantees offered. Readers are cautioned to rely on their own judgment about their individual circumstances to act accordingly. While all attempts have been made to verify information provided in this publication, the Publisher assumes no responsibility for errors, omissions, or contrary interpretation of the subject matter herein. Any perceived slights of specific persons, peoples, or organizations are unintentional.

This book is not intended for use as a source of legal, business, accounting or financial advice. All readers are advised to seek services of competent professionals in legal, business, accounting and finance fields.

The author and the publisher do not warrant that the information contained in this book is fully complete or comprehensive in any way.

Introduction

When it comes to life and business, it is no coincidence that some people always seem to fail while others always seem to flourish. For sure, chance plays a role in everything. But as individuals, as business-owners, as thinkers, and as parents/spouses, we have a significant degree of control over our lives.

Now, we can use the control that we have to influence outcomes in bad ways... Or we can use it to influence outcomes in our favor and in the favor of those we care about most.

When we use it poorly or when we don't use it at all, it should come as no surprise that our outcomes are bad. And when we use it thoughtfully and carefully, it should come as no surprise when we succeed.

For the majority of my life, since about the age of 16, I have felt incredibly lucky, blessed, and grateful. I found myself in situations repeatedly where I wanted something, believed it could happen, thought about it, and manifested it to be a reality in my life.

Here are three examples of situations that come to mind:

4. In high school, I went to a college welcome weekend and saw the cutest boy there. I thought, "Man, I hope I meet him when we start school!" I forgot all about it, and after moving into the dorms, I saw him on my floor. Apparently, he was very good friends with my neighbors across the hall. He would come up and watch the Chapelle Show with our friends, and then one day.. he asked me out on a date. It didn't turn into anything, as we didn't seem too compatible. However, it's one of the early experiences that made me realize that I am just very lucky and blessed.
5. In early 2018, I was making $36k per year, working for a retirement company. I am a hard worker and a fast learner, and I knew that I could make a living that was more comfortable for my family. I stayed positive, kept working, and stayed focused on becoming a six-figure earner. In 2023, I got a raise and was making $115k at my day job. Meanwhile, I had 4 side businesses with my boss that were generating additional revenue and getting us prepared for early retirement.
6. In 2020, I started a business with a partner. We built a temporary staffing company and bought a commercial property to rent out. In 2023, we decided to leap into online sales. We opened an Amazon store, started publishing books with Kindle, and started selling digital books and training courses. In the past year, we have scaled our business to earn 7 figures and average at least 6 figure months for the last 18 months!

Fortunately for you, this book is all about the things I have learned as I experienced situations listed above and how I kept pushing to grow a 7 figure business.

It's about changing your life for the better by making sound decisions and eliminating limiting beliefs. If you're experiencing bad outcomes when there's no reason to, we need to ensure that this problem stops.

Most importantly, this book is about success. It is about extracting the characteristics of others that make them successful at work, in parenthood, in their relationships, in the gym, or in the workplace... and then adopting those characteristics for your own use.

So, without further ado, let's take the plunge.

Section #1: Success in Business Management & Growth

Today, you will stop telling yourself that you have no control over your life. Today, you will learn exactly what it means to take that control, grasp it firmly, and use it to achieve success in all areas of your life.

In this section, I will provide you with tips for achieving success in business. It doesn't matter whether you own a business, want to own a business, or play an important managerial role. There are certain traits and habits that you can adopt that will determine whether or not you can be successful in the long run.

One important part of success is responsibility. Those who accept responsibility for their actions feel empowered to make changes. Those who cannot accept responsibility when it comes to how they navigate the world will never fully understand how much they can create change in their own lives. They will often blame others for shortcomings and be more likely to give up in the face of adversity.

If you look at the world around you, you'll quickly notice that some people are successful with money and others are not. Some find ways to get and hold good jobs and to get promoted within those jobs. Some do not.

Again, it's no surprise that we see these differences. What is important is that we learn from these differences and find out how we can get better at obtaining what we desire in life… getting good jobs, getting good promotions, and managing our finances better.

Here are some principles that have helped me find and maintain success and happiness in life.

Principle #1 – Stop Complaining

When it comes to success and business, the best place to start is by committing yourself to not complaining.

Of course, it is perfectly fine to raise concerns, to question dubious choices, and to remain thoughtful & analytical.

However, needless and persistent complaining accomplishes nothing positive. In fact, it often does the opposite. It drags you down, reflects poorly on you, and can transform otherwise productive people around you into cynical, whining, unproductive people as well.

In short, I want you to focus on solving problems, not complaining that they cannot be solved.

If you have a solution focused approach to situations, you will often be able to navigate your life without feeling like everything is a problem. It just feels like another task, another to-do, or another goal.

Principle #2 – Strive to Reach Your Full Potential

One of the things that prevents many people from achieving the best possible outcomes in their lives is complacency.

Once they begin to do well at something in business, at work, in their relationship, in the gym — they start to slack off. They take a mini mental or physical vacation from the grind.

Instead of ratcheting things up further, they let things play out and stop contributing to the growth and consistency that breeds success. Usually, the end result of this is regression.

Instead of becoming complacent, push hard to reach your full potential at every turn.

Brainstorm. Have planning sessions. Set goals. Keep the drive alive.

Principle #3 – Limit Your Use of Short Cuts

Of course, some short cuts are a good thing. If you can find a way to go from point A to point B in half of the time and there is no downside to the new route, then you should of course take it.

But in many cases (especially in business), we face tradeoffs.

Example: We might be able to cut costs by waiting to give employees a raise, and as a result, they may become disgruntled and intentionally shirk their duties.

If you see one that's good and doesn't appear to have a downside, then seize it. I am all about working smarter and not harder. Efficiency is the   Just be cautious and avoid the easy way out if it will yield less impactful results.

Principle #4 – Be a Continuous Learner

People have different learning styles. Some learn all the time and find ways to incorporate that learning into their lives. These people are continuous learners.

On the other hand, most people learn in tiny chunks. For example, they might find out how to use a new software program, but immediately after doing so, will cease to learn anything new about it until it is absolutely necessary.

In general, those who learn in chunks often find themselves at a serious disadvantage, as they often neglect to learn many of the important factors, products, people, and tools they interact with on a daily basis. Things are not in depth. They rarely take the time to become extraordinary in a task or topic.

So, try to be a continuous learner. It may be difficult, but you'll be happy you made the switch.

Approaching situations with curiosity and an eagerness to learn allows room for excitement, creativity, innovation, and improvement.

Principle #5 – Always Have a Plan, Even if You Don't Use It

Some people plan their lives to an outstanding degree. For each minute of the day, they have something scheduled. Like clockwork, their days play out with very few unforeseen events.

Initially, you might think this sounds boring, but in business, it is the status quo among those who are most successful.

It helps you to avoid decision fatigue. If you can avoid making decisions about small, routine, and tedious things, you can save your mental strength for bigger and more productive efforts.

This plan may be related to your daily schedule. It may be related to your goal planning. Just remember, even if you don't opt to use your plan, at least you will have the option to do so and can easily fall into a success groove.

This maximizes results.

Principle #6 – Don't Dwell on the Past

It's impossible to go throughout a career or a rich life without hitting a number of bumps in the road. No matter how hard you try, no matter how thoughtful you are, you are bound to hit some snags here and there.

And when you do hit those snags, your reaction to them will always influence your capacity for success. You can either learn from them, move on, and continue working to reach your goal, or you can dwell on them, allowing them to drag you down at every step of the way.

No matter how bad any failure was, it's over. All you can do now is work carefully to improve your future prospects. Wallowing in misery will not bring joy or success.

Learning from mistakes allows for correction. Dwelling on them can slow your momentum and create interference.

Principle #7 – Give Up When It's Wise to Do So, Not When it Is Convenient

Most people give up for reasons of convenience. They hit a nasty snag in their career or in their relationship, and they simply cannot find a way to get what they want immediately, so they just give up.

Instead of backing off, consulting a colleague/friend, and then heading back to the problem with a refreshed perspective, they give up before they give the scenario the chance to play out.

As a result, they deny themselves the opportunity to fight back and succeed.

Quitting based on facts if one thing, but quitting because of frustration, stress, fear, or fatigue is something completely different.

Making decisions based on facts and faith will often lead to much greater results.

Principle #8 – Listen to Those Around You

One common trait among those who are successful is that they listen to others and work to understand them. Instead of seeing everyone around them as inferior fools with nothing to contribute, they understand that most good ideas come from other people—not from them. If you want to be successful, too, you should follow this practice carefully in your daily business relations.

Collaboration and idea sharing has led to many of the greatest creations of our time. One person cannot be an expert in everything. In addition, having the humility to understand others' value decreases judgement and increases curiosity. Curiosity leads to innovation. Innovation attracts interest.

How many business owners succeed and make money without clients or customers? ZERO

We must always remember to recognize the needs of others, the desires of others, and the fact that we cannot make money without having someone buy what we are selling. Without others, we cannot maintain success in business. Hear people out. Work to best meet your client's needs, and maintain appreciation of how valuable they are to your success.

Principle #9 – Have Patience

One of the most common traits among those who are successful in business is patience. Those who lack patience frequently find themselves trapped in plans developed by those who have it... or rushing themselves into a situation that is less than ideal.

Developing patience allows time for forethought. It allows time to make decisions based on the greatest long term success, rather than based on frustration, impulsivity, or irritability. If you are stressed or overwhelmed, take a step back or a break. Allow yourself an opportunity for a mental recovery.

Use wisdom when making decisions. This will be the best way to find continued forward progress that is in alignment with your goals.

Principle #10 – Don't Settle

In some cases, you will find that the deck is stacked against you and your plans; you will simply have to settle with the best you can get. But in most situations, this simply isn't the case.

Don't find reasons to settle when you don't have to.

Instead, push hard and persistently for the best you can get. Enhance your options and possibilities as much as you can. While there are some things that will be beyond your control, fighting for the best case scenario will almost certainly lead to better results than settling.

Mediocrity and inadequate results can be overcome, if you continue to put energy into getting something better.

Principle #11 – Create Opportunities—Don't Wait for Them

Many people who have not achieved success in business are under the impression that opportunities arrive passively. All they have to do is wait for one to show up on the front door and then grab it.

More often, successful business owners and managers know that opportunities are usually created, not stumbled over. So make an effort to create opportunities in your daily work.

No one has ever handed me $100k after working for them for four months. However, I have earned $100k in four months and taken large distributions from my own business. I created this scenario, fought for it, put in the work.

You will be your own greatest representative in the world. How you network, devote energy into learning, create business opportunities, nurture relationships… all of it impacts how you bring opportunity to your life.

Principle #12 – Keep the Big Picture in Mind, But Stay Focused on the Short-Term Process

The big picture is important. It tells you where you are and where you're going. However, in some situations, it can distract you from the task at hand.

If you want to attain true success, then you have to know how to stay focused and effective in working with short-term problems and goals while also working within the greater framework of the big picture.

If you only focus on the big picture, it can be easy to become overwhelmed.

If you take small steps toward your goal as time goes by, it can help you to make more long-term progress and help prevent burnout/mental fatigue.

Principle #13 – Record Your Progress

Identifying and recording progress is important. It tells you how far you've come from where you once where. If you don't follow it carefully, it's easy to miss that it has occurred at all.

So, as progress occurs, record it somewhere. Write down exactly what happened, why it qualifies as "progress," and why you think it happened.

This will help you to keep your morale strong as you experience hurdles.

As you work to maintain positivity, remember that it can be easy to focus more on hiccups than highlights. Do not let these overshadow the good.

Even small strides can lead to big results over time.

Principle #14 – Record Your Failures

Similar to recording your progress, record your failures, too.

No matter how bad a failure was, force yourself to think hard about it. Reflect to see what you could have done better and how your approach may need to be modified.

Ask yourself what went wrong. Consider whether that was something you could influence or if chance or other factors played an important role in determining the outcome.

As painful as this process might be, it will help you to process your failures and to assimilate the lessons you take from them into future business decisions.

It prevents you from spinning your wheels, which can be very dangerous for new business owners. Spinning wheels burn gas and get you no where. Wasted energy and time can lead to burnout, which is a leading cause of giving up.

Learn from failures to avoid quitting for the wrong reasons. If something can be overcome, let's overcome it.

Principle #15 – Do Not Allow Hope to Overcome Analysis

Hope is an important emotional driver of actions. It can motivate you to continue on a path, even when you know the road ahead is difficult. However, in some situations, we simply allow hope to take over and ignore the consequences.

If you want to be truly successful, then it is wise to practice "cautious optimism," rather than chasing hope regardless of what your brain tells you.

Evaluate what works and what does not. Use this to guide your decision making, rather than just using blind optimism.

Principle #16 – Develop Good Habits

Habits are things that stick with you and drive your behavior, even when you aren't thinking about them. For this reason, it is important to try to develop good ones, such as responding to clients and customers in a timely manner, being consistently courteous, and facing challenges head-on, rather than slinking into the background.

Wake up early, pray, work out, spend time recharging your batteries, work to stay organized, identify your goals and daily action steps to take working toward them… these things and many more can impact your future success.

Show me how you do one thing, and it shows how you do everything. If you invest in success, you can achieve it.

Principle #17 – Identify and Rid Yourself of Bad Habits

No matter who you are and how successful you have been, you're probably carrying at least a couple of bad habits.

Perhaps you procrastinate. Or perhaps you become indecisive when the going gets tough. No matter what it is that you struggle with, identify your bad habits, so you can work to eliminate them from your life.

Changing a habit is not always easy, but with awareness and effort, they can be changed.

Principle #18 – Write Down Your Ideas and Others'
Just because you're no longer a professional student doesn't mean you should stop taking notes.
Next time you or someone else says something that is truly insightful or useful, jot it down as a note.
In the long run, this will save you time and money, as you won't have to waste precious time rediscovering your own and others' insights.
This can also help to guide your goal accomplishment and help contribute to you working smarter, not harder.
Put any pride to the side and be grateful when others' ideas help you to flourish.

Principle #19 – Set Goals
This simple fact cannot be emphasized enough: one thing that separates successful people from those who are not successful is goals.
The successful people have goals, and these goals give them meaning and direction.
If you're lacking serious, meaningful goals, then you should spend some time to create them and then write them down. Develop a plan. It can help to guide you when you feel stuck.
Reviewing your goals and why you established them to begin with can also help to motivate you when the going gets tough. It will help you to continue pushing toward success.

Principle #20 – When It's Time to Be Serious, Be Serious
One thing that separates successful people from those who have not yet experienced success is the ability to become serious or focused when it is important.
Many people simply cannot do this. Instead, when they are faced with real problem that feels unsolvable, they use humor, procrastination, or some other device to shy away from the problem.
If you want to be truly successful, you must learn to get serious when it's time to be serious. Where you invest your time, energy, and money impacts your life in massive ways.
You want to ensure that this investment brings value, so take it seriously.

Principle #21 – Seize the Moment
Another important quality that the successful have is their ability to seize the moment. When they see an opportunity in arm's length and they know that it's real, they take it. They don't debate it for a month until it is too late.
You will need to shift your thinking from, "I cannot afford to spend my time or money on that" to "How can I afford not to seize this opportunity?"
This does not mean that you should chase everything and spread yourself too thin. It just means that maintaining an open mind is what helps successful people see the opportunities and possibilities that are in front of them.

Principle #22 – Don't Just Learn, Apply Knowledge
When it comes to business, "learning" isn't enough.
In business, learning is only as valuable as the return it generates.
This is why you must get in the habit of learning new things—and then applying them immediately.

Many of us have heard the phrase, "use it or lose it."

This applies in business as well. If you go to a training on budget development or tax preparation and you wait six months to apply what you have learned, it is likely that you will have wasted six months of time with a poor budget or disorganized financial records. In this scenario, why would you go to a budget or tax prep seminar? It is likely because you thought it would help you.

If you see the value, maximize your use of the value. Do it quickly, so you can avoid wasting time and resources on something that gets pushed to the side or forgotten.

Principle #23 – Take Time to Think About & Evaluate Important Decisions

Most people agree that "analysis paralysis" is a bad thing. However, when it comes to making decisions, we often err too far on one side or the other. Sometimes, we take far too long. Other times, we don't take long enough.

Instead of deliberating carefully, forming an opinion, and then acting, we may end up jumping to a conclusion or wasting endless days thinking about the subject.

In the end, our interests are better served by making the decision fast, but doing so based on sound information.

Principle #24 – Avoid the Unnecessarily Extravagant

Creativity is important, but when it is excessive, it can lead to complexity. The successful know that being over the top is not often useful.

Rather, it can often turn into a form of day-dreaming that does not translate into practical and reasonable set of steps you can take to improve your situation.

Getting information, resources, and services out to your clients will help to keep your business moving forward. If you decide to sit in your basement alone for 9 months, working on the perfect masterpiece that you can share with the world, that is fine.

However, I tend to lean more toward the mentality that DONE IS BETTER THAN PERFECT.

When I present something to my clients, I would rather get them pieces of information that they can take to go grow their business fast than flood them with everything I have done in the past 10 years to start and run a multi-million dollar business.

Sometimes, we have to remind ourselves that simplicity will help our business and clientele more than bragging and showing some sort of extravagance.

Principle #25 – Think in Terms of Problems and Solutions

Those who are successful in most of their endeavors see the world in terms of problems and solutions. When they hit a bump in the road, they go into problem-solving mode, rather than going into problem-avoidance mode or panicking.

When you remain calm and approach problems with a problem-solving mindset, you are more likely to make rational decisions that are based on logic and reason rather than emotions. Panic can cloud your judgment and lead to poor decision-making.

By staying calm, you can approach the problem methodically, analyze it from different angles, and channel your energy into finding a solution. You can also inspire confidence in others and help guide them through difficult situations.

Mindset is an important variable that we can all influence. No matter whether it comes to personal relationships or business transactions, improving our focus and acting intentionally can bring about a positive effect.

Principle #26 – Delegate Tasks to Others

If you ever want to match the success of some of your heroes, you will need to learn how to delegate tasks to others. Successful people are willing and able to break down a large task and to efficiently and intelligently allocate its pieces to themselves or others, ensuring completion of the task and steady progress toward reaching a goal.

If there are many tasks in front of you, managing your time and priorities will become increasingly important. I want you to evaluate whether you should:

Do it – the task requires attention now

Ditch it – this task will have little positive impact on the business. Drop it, and move on. Don't let it get you stuck.

Delegate it – Can a freelancer, employee, or other partner get this done better and faster than you can? It may be worth your time to delegate this to others.

Delay it – This can have a profound positive impact on your business, but it is a time consuming project, and you don't have time for it right now.

When done successfully, task management and time management breed success. Going forward, try to prioritize your work. Try to determine which projects are "urgent," which projects are "important," and which projects are both. And then attack them in the correct order.

Principle #27 – Correct Your Weaknesses

Another important trait of the successful is their ability to identify and correct weaknesses, gradually working to overcome them and build strength in these areas.

For instance, if they recognize that they are particularly weak at decision-making, then they will make an effort to become decisive, rather than pondering the situation for long periods of time or wallowing in anger about problems.

Continuous improvement and evaluation of pain spots help successful people to jump over hurdles, rather than tripping on them and falling to the ground.

Those who are stubborn and refuse to see the errors in their ways will often repeat them in their personal and professional lives.

Principle #28 – Don't Let Emotions Get the Best of You

Emotions can be an important driver of success.

They can keep you focused on a goal, and they can support your discipline to go on, even when things start to look bleak.

Unfortunately, emotions can also play a deeply negative role when it comes to running a business.

They can guide you into making irrational, impulsive, vindictive, and poorly thought-out choices.

Sadly, this can also lead to wasting resources. With many small businesses failing in the first two years, this is a very important consideration.

Evaluation will often lead you to more success than emotion, so don't let your emotions get the best of you.

Allow them push you on toward success.

Principle #29 – Be Humble and Honest
Two additional traits that many successful individuals share are humility and honesty.
Honesty is crucial for building trust. This helps to establish credibility and foster strong relationships with customers.
When business owners are honest about challenges, mistakes, and shortcomings, they demonstrate a willingness to continuously learn, grow, and improve their skills.
Humility and honesty contribute to a strong reputation, loyal customer base, and motivated workforce, all of which are essential for sustainable growth and success.
In business, opportunities abound to make questionable decisions from which you can profit. This might involve lying about your product or tricking your co-workers. In general, successful people know not to go this route, but instead to focus on making money legitimately and in a way that doesn't harm or trick others.

Principle #30 – Always Improve Your Business Processes
Along with being a continuous learner, you should try to be a continuous improver, too.
Wherever your business is lacking, make it better.
Wherever you see room for improvement, make one.
Analyze and evaluate your systems, to see what can be enhanced or cleaned up.
Evaluate which services and products are most beneficial to your employees.
As time goes by, this will help you to avoid spending time on things that do not actually help your bottom line or lead to positive results for the business.

Principle #31 – Create Networks with Other Business Owners
Another important part of success in business is networking with other managers and business owners.
Find out how they run their businesses. See whether you can learn from them or work with them in some complementary fashion. See if you can collaborate or learn from each other.
Learning from others will often lead to better results than resenting them will.

Principle #32 – Do Not Allow Your Personal Life to Interfere with Your Business Life
No matter what is going in on your personal life, remember to keep work at work and home at home, as much as possible.
Don't allow a stressful situation with a friend or a relative spill over into your work and prevent you from being effective or making forward progress.
As a perk, when your business is successful, it often grants you the flexibility to focus more on your family or home life.
I just want you to do your best to avoid letting personal stressors prevent you from seeing professional growth.

Principle #33 – Be Fast
One important trait of successful individuals in business is that they know that speed is important.
Often, starting earlier and moving faster can make the difference between profitability and closing your doors.

So keep this in mind next time you are lagging far behind your competitors and cannot decide whether or not to push ahead or continue stagnating.

Keep this in mind when you set time frames for responding to clients or vendors. We live in a fast paced world. If you do not meet their needs, someone else will.

Principle #34 – Differentiate Yourself from Competitors

Whether you are competing for a promotion at work or competing with another business, differentiating yourself from your competitors is usually a good idea. It helps you to stand out in a world where so many people are trying to sell something or get the same opportunity you are after.

Your goal should always be to spell out to either your boss or your customers (whichever case is the relevant one) that you have certain qualities that are desirable.

This will often help you to draw the right type of attention without having to say anything about other businesses or your co-workers.

Principle #35 – Leave Your Comfort Zone

When it comes to business, it is easy to settle into your comfort zone and stop taking risks, stop innovating, and stop creating new products or expanding your services.

In some cases, if your comfort zone is a good place to be, your results may be very good. However, if you are experiencing a decline in hitting your goals, then it may be time to leave your comfort zone.

Challenge yourself to enhance your product or service offering, and give your clients the feeling that they need you again.

Principle #36 – Be Persistent

In business, few things are more closely related to success than persistence. Persistence will determine whether you push ahead or give up altogether. Persistence will determine whether you eventually break through as a leader in your field or whether you allow everyone else to walk over you to get to the top. Being resourceful and finding ways to continue toward success can be a major factor that sets you apart from others in the crowd.

Remember that taking one step each day for a year will get you further than taking zero steps each day for 100 years.

Principle #37 – Give Things Time to Get Better (or Worse)

In many situations, it is tempting to micromanage the implementation of a project. It can also be tempting to give up when you approach a hurdle, rather than to jump over it.

You may feel the need to analyze what's going on and make repeated changes. However, it is important to know when enough is enough and when it might just be best to give things time to play out before making a change.

Flipping everything upside down or dropping it completely may not be as beneficial as building on it and enhancing it gradually, over time.

You do not always need to act with haste. Sometimes, it is helpful to really think through your next move before making it or to weigh your options before selecting the best one.

Principle #38 – Be Realistic with Yourself and Others

One thing that successful people know is that being realistic with yourself and others is crucial.

In a business environment, if you do not tell others when they may be mistaken, they will continue on the wrong path. And if you do not allow others to correct you, then you will do the same.

Making sure that you approach others with respect is critical to successfully communicating your needs.

Making sure that you are receptive to feedback and do not respond to it with defensiveness will also help others to feel that you are approachable and will keep the doors to communication open.

Remember, consultation and communication are key to success. Two heads are better than one, so being able to share ideas will often lead to the swiftest and most beneficial results.

Principle #39 – Take Action Immediately

Thoughts and actions are two very different things.

This is something successful people know very well.

They know that coming up with a good idea is completely useless if you cannot implement it—or cannot give it to someone who can.

Get in the habit of not only thinking of new things, but of taking action swiftly. Turn ideas into reality.

Principle #40 – Become Goal-Oriented

Don't only set goals but become goal-oriented. That is, in every waking moment, decide how you will channel your energy and actions toward outcomes that favor your chosen set of goals.

There is going to be a noticeable difference in your life when you shift from writing goals on paper and then looping back around to check on them every few months to writing your goals on paper, accomplishing them, creating more, and accomplishing those too.

Being goal oriented keeps you constantly moving in the direction of your immediate and your long term goals.

Principle #41 – Use Visualization Techniques

Visualization techniques can be very powerful instruments for achieving goals in business.

Next time you hit a rough patch of uncertainty, consider spending some time visualization how you will behave in order to get through it. This will not only relax you, but it will also prepare you for the road ahead.

The power of the mind is nothing to underestimate. If you do not believe that you can accomplish your goals, you are more likely to give up on them before they are reached.

Principle #42 – Work on Your Time Management Skills

If you want to be successful, time management is vital. Not only must you keep track of all of your appointments, meetings, and project deadlines, but you also must manage your time when it comes to accomplishing tasks.

If you allocate too much time to a project, that's time that you cannot use for a different project. It is important to look at things and consider what priority they have in your to-do list.

You could find yourself constantly working, but if you are working in a disorganized or inefficient way, you are going to feel like you are spinning your wheels, always working and never reaping the rewards or getting a chance to feel rested.

You must prioritize working smarter, NOT HARDER, to avoid burn out.

If you have a team, remember to consult with them or lean on them for support, to avoid taking all of the burdens on yourself and trying to look like a hero, at the expense of your mental health or wellness.

Principle #43 – Organize Your Workspace

Having a clean, organized workspace is a vital part of success. It may sound trivial, but in fact, the cleanliness and the order can go a long way towards improving your mindset and structuring your day.

If things look organized, they are more likely to feel organized. This can also help you to move more seamlessly from one task to another, if things are clearly laid out and organized.

Principle #44 – Create Schedules and Use a Calendar

Similar to keeping your office space clean and organized, keeping your schedule clean and organized is important, too. It helps to keep your mind clear of unnecessary clutter and worries.

It helps you to keep your focus on what must be accomplished by outlining what you need to focus on in this moment.

This helps to reinforce mental organization and time management for all of your to-dos.

In business, efficiency is prized. It's not enough to simply do something well, you must also do it well and fast. Successful people do this, and you should, too.

Principle #45 – Take Control of Your Role in the Business

When it comes to business, staying in control means a lot.

It means that you not only prevent other businesses from dictating an agenda for you, but it also means that you firmly seize control of your own destiny. If you want to be successful, then you must be willing to take control. You cannot be afraid to address people, share the value of what you have to offer, and truly guide your own success.

Principle #46 – Be Analytical About Your Results

In business, analysis is important. If something goes wrong, there are reasons for why it went wrong. Using a careful, well-reasoned approach is the best way to determine what those reasons were. So, instead of trying to mentally avoid the problems altogether, focus on the process of analyzing your problems and working to obtain more favorable results.

Principle #47 – Stop Doing Things that Don't Work

From time to time, you will determine that things don't work… or at least they don't work as well as they should. When this happens, you can take one of two paths. The first path ignores the problem and hopes that things get better. The second puts an end to it by modifying your approach. Stop doing the things that are not working. If you want to be successful, you will learn to have the courage and insight to do the latter of these two options.

Principle #48 – Find Out Which Forms of Advertising Generate Revenue And Which Do Not

In business, marketing can do a lot to transform your business.

It can expand the audience for your product, persuade the existing audience, or it can provide no benefits at all while incurring massive costs.

Those who are successful in business pay attention to their advertising, so they can determine which forms are beneficial and which forms should be discontinued.

Please do not waste money on ads to buy customers when you have not established a reputation that will help others to trust you. A lot of money can be wasted very quickly, if you do not have the social evidence that you have something to offer your customers.

Try to get testimonials, followers, social media engagement, positive reviews… anything that can serve as evidence that you are trusted in your niche.

Principle #49 – Always Consider the Possibility that You Are Wrong

No one person can be an expert in everything. In some situations, you could make mistakes or be wrong about things. This is simply the nature of business. Instead of declaring your opinions or judgements and getting indignant, open yourself up to the possibility that you have made an error.

Principle #50 – Keep Things Simple

Simplicity is often underrated. In fact, many business owners are prone to believing that if something is simple, then it cannot be true. They believe the world is a complex place, so solutions to a problem in business cannot be simple. In fact, many of the more successful innovations in business are simple. So, think twice before you taking things up a notch in terms of complexity. Instead, think about using solutions that are simple, elegant, communicable, and likely to work.

Principle #51 – When Failure Arrives, Accept it, Learn from It, and Move On

Often, in business, we encounter many failures before we encounter a success. If we don't make an effort to determine why we are failing and how we might turn that failure into a success, it's possible that we'll never emerge with the success. Rather, we would be likely to repeat these failures.

Principle #52 – Inspire Confidence in Those Around You

Rather than tearing down your fellow co-workers, make every attempt possible to build them up. Having a confident staff around you will multiply the returns you reap from your own efforts.

Principle #53 – Do Not Compete with Your Staff; Help Them and Learn How They Can Help You

Being successful means being secure. And being secure means that you don't feel the need to compete with your co-workers, but instead focus on competing with other businesses.

Principle #54 – Avoid Becoming Discouraged Easily

One important difference between those who are successful and those who are not is that the successful do not get discouraged easily. No matter how poorly things appear to be going, they find a way to stick through things until the end. If you want to become successful, you should try to emulate this behavior.

Principle #55 – Adopt the Habits of Successful Individuals

Do you know someone at work who is very successful at what they do? Observe their behavior and try to copy it. If they approach problem solving in a particular way, copy that approach and make it your own. If they have a certain routine that they adhere to religiously, then adopt that, too. Successful people observe behaviors of others and try to implement best practices into their own routines.

Principle #56 – Facilitate Discussion
Another important trait of business leaders who are successful is their ability to facilitate discussion. Not only do they have good ideas themselves, but they find ways to tease good ideas out of otherwise quiet co-workers.

Principle #57 – Ask Stupid Questions if You Really Don't Know the Answer
People sometimes say that "there is no such thing as a stupid question." When it comes to making decisions that will determine the fate of your business, this is true. If you don't know the answer to a question, you should ask, find out the answer, and make your decision based on the accurate and complete information.

Principle #58 – Learn and Practice the Fundamentals
If you find that your business ideas and practices are not producing good results, then you should do what the successful do and return to the fundamentals. Think hard about what sound business principles would dictate, and practice that, rather than constantly attempting to innovate.

Principle #59 – Always Ask for Comments (Good or Bad)
Thick skin is a valuable asset in business. It means not only having the ability to listen to and accept praise and as well as insults and critical comments. If you want to be successful in business, you must have thick skin and you must always ask for comments—be they good or bad.

Principle #60 – Avoid Getting Irrationally Defensive
Becoming defensive is a natural response to getting cornered, think fight or flight. Instead of opening up to criticism and accepting suggestions, we start shooting down any comment directed at us, be it useful or not. If you want to be successful in business, you must resist the urge to become defensive.

Principle #61 - Cultivate a Willingness to Succeed in Those Around You
Business culture is driven by the network in which it is embedded. If you want to cultivate a culture of success and confidence, then you must be sure that you exude confidence and success and inspire it in others.

Principle #62 – Don't Hang Your Hat on Delusional Visions of Overnight Success
While it can be comforting to dream big about your future, having delusions about your success is purely detrimental. It will cause you to set unreasonable goals and attempt to live up to unrealistic expectations.

Principle #63 – Affirm Yourself and Your Choices
In business, you will have to make many difficult decisions. Instead of constantly second-guessing your decisions, take time to affirm your choices periodically, so that you do become overwhelmed by self-doubt.
When it comes to business, few things are more important than decisiveness. But what's important to understand is that decisiveness doesn't simply mean making decisions fast. It means knowing how to make good decisions fast. If you don't do this now, make it a point to get better at it.

There is a time to be humble.
When you are showcasing your skills in business and striving for success, it is also important to move forward with confidence about your expertise

Principle #64 – Find Time to Give Yourself a Break
In addition to working hard, the successful know to take breaks, too. Without breaks, we have no way to clear our minds, re-energize, and prepare for the task that faces us.

Principle #65 – Create a Product that People Actually Want to Buy
One thing you don't hear often from successful people is how they swindled a bunch of people into buying a low-quality product for a high-price. To the contrary, they will usually regale you with stories of how they beat competitors by offering a lower price or a better product.

Principle #66 – Keep Your Customers' Best Interests at Mind
Following the general theme of the previous tips, keeping your customers' best interests in mind is vital. It will not only keep you focused on creating products that they'll appreciate and use, but it will also keep you satisfied with your job.

Principle #67 - Streamline Your Business Processes
No matter how efficient you think your business is managed, there are almost always opportunities for improvement. It's just a matter of finding these opportunities and using them to streamline how your business functions.

Principle #68 - Do Not Ask too Much of Your Employees
You might be tempted to squeeze every last cent out of your employees, but instead consider what the successful often do: they try to keep costs low, but at the same time, when they need talent, they pay for it. Keep this in mind when hiring and when giving raises.

It's also important to the culture you create in your workplace. When people are overworked or taken for granted, it can make them feel unappreciated and create unnecessary turnover for business owners.

Treat people with dignity and respect. Try not to let all of the pressure that may be on you effect those around you

Principle #69 - Learn to Deal with and Overcome Stress
In business, stress is inevitable. Competition is everywhere and it isn't always obvious what you should do in order to win. If you want to be successful, you have to learn how to cope with stress and how to prevent it from dragging you down.

Principle #70 – Improve Your Written and Verbal Communication
Many who are successful and frequently get promoted in the workplace have powerful written communication skills. If yours are lacking, consider taking an English class or studying to enhance skills.

Verbal communication is a vital ingredient of success. Without being able to clearly communicate your ideas to others, you will have a tough time being a strong leader. If you don't yet have this skill, you may want to consider taking a public speaking class.

Principle #71 - Make Friends and Allies
When it comes to being successful in the workplace, few things are more important than having a group of friends and allies who can say good things about

you to the higher-ups. So make an effort to be social, make friends, and have lunch with your co-workers.

Principle #72 – Put in Extra Time at the Office Occasionally
Successful people know that being dedicated to your job isn't enough. You must also demonstrate that dedication to your employer. One way in which you can do this is by staying late when your employer is also staying late, so she can observe you working and gain a positive impression.

Principle #73 - Be the First to Volunteer for Undesirable Projects
One easy way to differentiate yourself from others at work is to always volunteer for projects that no one else wants to do. Sure, it'll be painful at first, but you'll quickly become recognized as an invaluable asset for the business. In addition, this will frequently help you to learn new skills and excel above others, who refuse to leave their comfort zones

Principle #74 - Volunteer to do Presentations
In many workplaces and businesses, presentations are a vital part of communicating ideas to employees, clients, and business partners. Unfortunately, many people fear presentations and often opt not to give them when given the choice. If you want to be successful, you should take every opportunity to give a presentation, speak to groups, and practice the art of captivating others.

Principle #75 – Don't Complain Frequently
When it comes down to it, a good manager or business owner knows that the buck stops at their desk. Instead of complaining about problems, they solve them. If you want to get promoted or grow your business, you must also take on this mindset. Groaning about problems is way less effective than working through them

Principle #76 - Try to Take the High Road
When it comes to petty, business or office disputes, always be the one to take the high road. Don't focus on getting revenge or supporting an argument that is clearly wrong. Instead, just admit fault and move on with your life. In some cases, when others are wrong, it is important to stand your ground and defend your position. However, in most cases, it is better for your success and the success of your business to swallow your pride and be the one to end an argument.
Peace breeds prosperity, if you allow it to.

Principle #77 - Avoid Jokes that Some Might Find Inappropriate or Offensive
Making jokes can endear others to you. However, making offensive or inappropriate jokes can permanently eliminate you from the running for upper management jobs or from winning over a potential client. Next time you go to make a joke, think twice about your audience. Keep it to yourself if you are worried that it might offend someone.

Principle #78 – Make an Effort to Appear & Be Stable
Stability is an important quality in individuals who are given a lot of responsibility. If they are unstable, they could make very bad decisions that jeopardize the entire business. For this reason, you should push very hard to demonstrate your stability to those around you. A lack of stability can crush any chance you had in building trust or authority with your audience.

Principle #79 - Collaborate When Asked

Teamwork is an essential component of success in any business endeavor. This is why it is essential that you learn how to collaborate with your peers and colleagues and practice it regularly. Avoid acting as though you are better than others.
Open up for collaborative opportunities. I've been telling my team this for years, and I want you to remember it, too:
Not one of us will go out and make $2 million dollars alone this year.
It is highly likely that you will have an assistant, a contracted writer, a web designer, an employee, a bookkeeper, or a consultant to help you along the way. Remember that more minds often leads to more success and innovation than just one Never underestimate the power of collaboration.

Principle #80 - Always Be Early or On Time

When you're late to a meeting, everyone notices. Whether this is your boss or a client, make a positive impression. Being on time or early shows others that you respect their time and that yours matters as well.

Imagine having other people keep you waiting. How does this cost you productivity? Yeah, it kills it!

If you're like me, you hate wasting your precious time and hate having others disregard the value of your time. Show others that you respect their time and want yours respected as well.

Principle #81 – Think and Contribute Critically

When you're at meetings or when a co-worker or boss asks for advice, think critically and try to make an important contribution. Don't let the words go in one ear and other the other. Be attentive to others, and provide them with creative and well thought out solutions and contributions.

Teach others how to excel to greater heights. Successful people don't fear scarcity. Instead, they embrace abundance. When they have knowledge and skills, they freely give it away to others with the understanding that those they help will become important allies in the future. Allies can attest to the strength of your reputation, which brings more success.

Principle #82 – Don't Sit Quietly at Meetings

If you want to be successful in the workplace, you cannot sit passively at meetings. Instead, you must take initiative and make comments. Get recognized, and make important contributions.

The only word of advice I have about being new is this. If I am newly invited to a meeting or am attending a conference for the first time, I usually spend the first meeting or first chunk of time evaluating what others are doing, the group dynamics, and how I may best support those around me before launching forward and taking things over.

Note. I said I "usually" do this. If you're the new facilitator, boss, or have another important reason to come in and take the lead, by all means, do so. Only hold back and evaluate group dynamics when time permits

Principle #83 – Empathize with Co-Workers and Higher-Ups

Empathy is important. Getting it from others makes you feel wanted and cared for. Giving it to others will improve your status within the company. It will show people that they can come to you if others do not understand their position. It also helps to create a soft cushion for people when you have to correct them or deliver bad news. They will understand that you have care for those around you and also must act responsibly on behalf of your company/team.

Principle #84 – Don't Make Enemies

Going back to touch on my prior point, if you want to be successful in the workplace, there's a good chance that you'll end up locking horns with a few people on the way. However, at the end of the day, it is vital that you don't take these disputes personally.

If all of your actions are centered around the success of your business and your team, you will always have a reasonable explanation for people who question what you are doing and your intentions. Act with integrity. Work hard to avoid making enemies. Your reputation is one of the most valuable things that you will build in your lifetime.

Principle #85 – Generate High-Quality Work

At the end of the day, the quality of work that you produce will determine whether your boss or client thinks that you are fit to carry out your current job. If they think you are over-qualified or outshine those around you, you are more likely to be promoted or get additional sales in your business. Demonstrating consistency in this area has helped me to be recruited by former colleagues to come serve as an executive for their company twice in my lifetime. It helped take me from the role of a job seeker to the one who is sought out. Never take for granted the power of your work ethic and reputation in the business world.

Principle #86 – Share Your Work and Ideas with Others

If you have good ideas, then share them with others. Let your co-workers, bosses, or clients benefit from your insights. Occasionally, you might get no credit for this, but over time, the praise you receive here and there will help to improve your status.

Principle #87 – Be Honest with Follow Co-Workers and Higher-Ups

Above all else, honesty is an important quality in the workplace. Being honest with your co-workers and your boss means that they can trust you and come to you for advice in the future.

Principle #88 – Be a Self-Starter

One of the most clearly identifiable traits of successful individuals is their ability to self-start. Instead of needing to be pushed around by bosses, they take action immediately and accomplish tasks on their own. If you want to get promoted or grow your own business, you should also get in the habit of doing this.

Principle #89 – Meet People and Make Friends

At least one a week, get out of your seat and walk the office. Meet the people who work next to you, and connect with them. When you're up for a promotion, it can never hurt to have too many friends.

Principle #90 – Expand Your Understanding of the Business

When it comes to getting a promotion, being good at your job isn't enough. In fact, it's just one prerequisite. In addition to being good at your job, you will also have to gain a much stronger understanding of the business you work in, so you can make broader, bigger picture suggestions.

Principle #91 – Don't Pass the Buck

Passing the buck is what you do if you don't want responsibility. If you want to be successful and to get promoted, don't pass the buck. Take any responsibility that comes your way and then ask for more.

Principle #92 – Don't Be Afraid to Stand-Up for Yourself
When it comes to contradicting your boss or a co-worker, you might decide that it is not a good idea to stand up for yourself, but instead to back-down. However, if you have good reason to believe you are right, you should stick up for yourself as long as it is reasonable and respectful. Ultimately, your co-workers and boss will respect you more for it.

Principle #93 – Become Deadline-Oriented
In the workplace, deadlines are everything. If you want to become successful, you must make it a point to follow deadlines very closely, so that your projects are always delivered on time. When deadlines are in place, do not permit yourself to fail in meeting them.

Principle #94 – Share Your Knowledge
In some cases, you will not be promoted directly, but will have to apply for a job within the company. In these cases, you will want to have a resume and portfolio (if applicable) available, so that you can use them in the interview.

Principle #95 – Rationalize Why You Are Worthy of a Promotion
Getting a promotion can be a difficult process. This is why it is important that you spend some time thinking about and rationalizing why you are worthy of a promotion. When the going gets tough, you'll have reasons that you can use to reinforce your choice.

Principle #96 – Don't Shy Away from Gray Areas
Gray areas are important. Those who are successful find out how to succeed, even when things are clearly black or white. Those who often fail to succeed cannot work through gray areas, but instead get confused and bogged down. If you want to get recognized and promoted, you must charge gray areas head-on and demonstrate that they won't make you ineffective.

Principle #97 – Don't Be an Apple-Polisher
Most bosses will appreciate it if you are kind and respectful to them, but if you go out of your way to suck up to them, it will usually be perceived poorly. Instead of respecting you, they will see you as someone they cannot trust for a straight answer.

Principle #98 – Perform a Gap Analysis
Perform a gap analysis of what you are missing today in order to be worthy of the promotion. Think exactly what things you will need to do in order to position yourself well for it.

Principle #99 – Master Your Job
Mastering your job won't be enough to get you a promotion, but it is without a question the best place to start. So, if you think there is significant room for improvement, then getting working to master your job.

Principle #100 – Stay Alert
Stay alert for important information about promotions and business opportunities. If you find these opportunities quickly and exploit them, you will greatly improve

your chances of gaining more success. Innovative ideas require swift action, if you want to get in on the ground floor.

Principle #101 – Dress for the Part

One important part of getting promotions is dressing for the part. If you don't look presentable on a daily basis, that may factor into your boss's decision not to promote you. So, dress for success.

I do not have to worry about this as a business owner, but when I worked for other people, I placed value on how I represented them. If you want to be promoted and have more responsibility placed on you, you must take it seriously. Being the face of another person's organization is a great responsibility.

Being the face of my own, this is also very important. However, my company values are also different. For example, if I am promoting comfort and a work life balance, it will not be quite so bad for me to be seen lounging around in a business promo. If I am showing the importance of fitness, it will be likely that I will be wearing athletic leisure apparel.

Your energy and look must support your goals.

Principle #102 – Create a Career Map

Create a map of your career that shows where you have been and where you want to finish your career (perhaps in upper management or perhaps as CEO). Along each step of the way, have a plan for how you will move from one spot to the next.

Principle #103 – Find a Good Mentor

One good way to find out how to lead and how to be successful is to get advice from a great mentor. This mentor could be your boss or could be a co-worker who is highly successful. Either way, find at least one mentor and try to get as much as you can get out of the relationship.

Similar to finding a mentor, try to follow people closely to get promoted. Ask yourself what qualities they have that ultimately make them so promotable. Then, try to copy those qualities

Pay attention to co-workers who are especially good at their jobs. What is it that enables them to be so efficient? And what is it that elicits so much praise from upper management? Copy these qualities and you should see the same results.

Principle #104 – Go Above & Beyond: Never Say "No"

One good way to demonstrate that you are responsible is to always say "yes" to difficult and unsavory projects. No matter how much you don't want to do them, accept them anyway and demonstrate that you are management material.

Whenever you are given a project at work, make it a point to over- deliver on all of the requirements. Make the boss appreciate your work and ensure they have a vested interest in promoting you.

Making a sacrifice for the company shows that you are interested in staying around longer. So, instead of trying to extract every last penny from the company while putting in as little work as possible, go the distance and prove that you are willing to make a sacrifice.

Principle #105 – Consider Why You Want the Promotion

Being prepared is important. For instance, next time you're in the elevator with your boss or with a higher-up, you will want to be prepared if your boss asks you something about a new job opening or a possible promotion. Have reasons ready for why you want the promotion and why you would fit well in the position.

Principle #106 – Be Scrappy
Scrappiness is an important trait of those who are successful. No matter how badly the road to success treats them, they take their lumps and then return to the path. Ultimately, they prevail because they refuse to do anything else.

Principle #107 – Make Your Boss Look Good
Another thing that the successful know how to do is to make the boss look good. This is especially true if you can do it in front of her superiors or a partner from another business. Your boss will appreciate this; and will want to do what she can to ensure that you are around to help her again.

Principle #108 – Befriend the HR Department
Make a friend in human resources. Next time there is a job opening in the works, you will be one of the first people to find out about it.

Principle #109 – Timing and Preparation are Important
When it comes to getting a promotion at work, few things are more important than timing. Being in the right place at the right time and saying the right things is vital. And this is why you must pay careful attention to your timing.

Ensure that someone else can do your job. If the no one can, then you cannot be replaced; and cannot get promoted.

Observe those who are in the position you are striving for. If they are already here, they clearly know how to be successful in your position. Take pointers, and implement them, to ensure that you are properly prepared for your next big step. In addition to simply being prepared for your promotion, you should also try to signal your preparedness and willingness to your superiors. Let them know that you would be interested in a promotion if one should become available.

Principle #110 – Don't Ask Questions if You Can Answer Them Yourself
One thing the successful do well is to solve problems themselves, rather than burdening others with them. If you want a promotion, you have to learn how to do this, too. Use resources to conduct research, rather than asking other people to research things for you, due to a lack of effort.

Principle #111 – Eliminate Turbulence in Your Personal Life
Turbulence in your personal life is bad for a lot of reasons, but one reason is that it can often spill-over into your work life, compounding the problem. So make every effort possible to reconcile with family members and to end fights quickly.

Principle #112 – Make Yourself Indispensable
If you can easily envision how the company could replace you, then your boss probably can, too. The successful know to make themselves indispensable, so that they are promoted or given a raise, rather than replaced.

Principle #113 – Learn How to be a Team Player
In essence, getting better at your job means getting better at playing your role on the team. Make an effort to demonstrate that you are a team player to your bosses; and you may be rewarded with an attempt to run that team.

Principle #114 – Learn New Skills & Strategies
One large part of getting promoted involves developing new skills. If you don't develop new skills, then you cannot expect that your boss will suddenly believe

that you are capable of taking on a new job with different requirements. In addition to acquiring new skills, you should also devise new strategies for tackling your current workload. Find ways to do it faster and better, so that you stand out more and can reap greater rewards in less time.

Principle #115 – Don't Try to Advance Prematurely
In the long run, your promotion should come naturally. It should come at a time when it is obvious to you and obvious to your bosses that you are interested and worthy. If you try to force the issue to quickly, it could backfire and negatively effect you in the long run.

Principle #116 – Maintain a Sense of Urgency
In all things you do at work, maintain a sense of urgency. Show that you are hard-working, attentive, and alert. And show that you won't become complacent simply because things are going well.

Principle #117 – Improve Your Profile within the Organization
Volunteer at charity events, help co-workers who are in need, and generally be available and helpful. As your profile improves within the company, so will your chances of getting promoted.

Principle #118 – Keep Your Boss in the Know
If there is something important that your boss needs to know, be the first to let her know about it. You will become someone that she can rely on for information, which will make you indispensable to the company.

Principle #119 – Apply for Within Company Jobs
Don't just passively wait for a promotion. Instead, do what the successful do and apply for within company jobs. Be aggressive about getting that promotion.

Principle #120 – Learn New Things
One way to make you indispensable to your company is to learn new things about your job. Work through a reference manual. Spend time learning how to use the company's proprietary software optimally. Do something that makes you better and more useful.

Principle #121 – Look for a Job Elsewhere
Find jobs outside of your company that look promising. At a minimum, you might be able to get a better job elsewhere. At most, you might be able to leverage that offer into a promotion within the company.

Principle #122 – Practice Self-Promotion
As painful as it might be at first, get in the habit of self-promoting (but in ways that don't make you look desperate or stupid). Get others to notice you and to appreciate what you do within the company.

Principle #123 – Maintain a Positive Outlook
No matter what line of work you're in, you're likely to run into a few bumps on the road. When you do, try to maintain a positive outlook on life. Often, this simple difference in mindset will determine the success or failure of a venture.

Principle #124 – Make Yourself Known at Conferences
In addition to making yourself known within the company, make yourself known outside of the company. Go to the relevant conferences for workers in your industry; and try to make a reasonable showing, so that people remember your name.

Principle #125 – Think Like a Leader
Instead of thinking like a worker who will never be promoted, think like a leader. Reflect this in your decisions and in your aura of confidence. Demonstrate to others that you can think on your feet and make important decisions; and you will be rewarded with promotions.

Section #2: How to be Successful with Money

This can be a tricky one, but it is so important. If you do not get your financial affairs in order when you are living as a middle-class citizen, it is not likely that you will get them in order with wealth.

We hear the horror stories all of the time. Someone hits the lottery, (some hit it big TWICE!) and they blow it all on extravagant parties, clothes, cars, jewelry, and more. Before you know it, they are broke again.

You can begin implementing simple strategies to help get you better prepared for future success and break old habits that may have contributed to cyclical struggles.

Principle #126 – Pay Off Your Debt

It cannot be emphasized enough. Unless you are young and are planning to get a number of very large raises in your lifetime, then you shouldn't be accumulating debt. You should be paying it down and saving for retirement or unexpected events. The successful know and practice this. Debt is often the product of delusion and wishful thinking. Instead of letting delusion run your life, drop the debt and get on a path to saving for a comfortable retirement.

Principle #127 – Start Saving Early

Start saving early. Investing $10,000 at age 30 will yield you much more in retirement than $10,000 invested at age 50. It is never too late to get started, so making efforts to increase savings will almost always get us better prepared for the future.

Principle #128 – Avoid Putting Yourself in a Precarious Financial Situation

The successful know that some risk is unavoidable, but where it is avoidable, it should be deal with intelligently. If you are constantly putting yourself in precarious financial situations, it may be time to rethink your finances and your approach to money.

We all go through hard times in our lives where the money isn't flowing. But when this is the case, you must cut back and live simply. Don't drive yourself into the ground financially, as the consequences are likely to manifest well into the future.

If you're currently over-budget, consider cutting your expenses by 10%. Even if it seems hard to do initially, try your best to figure it out and do it.

Principle #129 – Keep Track of Your Finances in a Spreadsheet and Follow a Budget

Instead of hoping that your finances will work themselves out, play a role in shaping your financial future by keeping track of everything in a spreadsheet. This is often the difference between success and failure in personal finance.

List out all of your bills on a spreadsheet. Start planning which paychecks need to cover which bills and how much you will need to set aside from each check, in order to cover all of your bills and necessities.

Budgets can play an important role in stabilizing financial outcomes. If you currently have no budget, you should start making one on a weekly basis. Try to keep your expenses and income flows under control, so you don't get behind on payments.

Principle #130 – Make an Effort to Cut Your Expenses

If your expenses are too high, then cut them. Move into a cheaper apartment. Buy bargains at the grocery store. Use coupons. Cut back on entertainment expenses. When you're trying to get your finances under control, thriftiness is a virtue. If you've fallen on hard times, you would be wise to be thrifty, rather than delusional about the state of your finances.

Principle #131 – Pay Your Bills on Time
When you miss a bill, you get charged fees. So, instead of paying your bills on the last day, pay them first. If you have money left over, then use it for other purposes, but don't do so until you have paid the bills.

Principle #132 – Set Financial Goals
Don't just dream about your finances getting better. Set financial goals and commit yourself to accomplishing them. This will keep you on track with your finances; and will give you something to look forward to.

Principle #133 – Invest in Your Career
Just like any other investment, an investment in your career could pay off considerably down the line. If you are currently missing the education or the training that you need to move forward in your career, then put some money aside to invest in your career.

Principle #134 – Consider Going Back to School or Getting Additional Training
If you're unsure of what to do on your current career path, then consider going back to school. Test the waters and figure out what it is that you want to do—or have an aptitude for; and then try again with a different career path.

Principle #135 – Keep Your Credit Card Balances Low or Paid When Possible
Try to keep your credit card balances under 30% of the total allowable limit. If there is some emergency, you will have a back up reserve of credit that you can use to get through it. If you can, pay your credit card balances in full each time you use them. This will prevent you from ever paying interest on the debt you are servicing.

Principle #136 – Shop Around for Insurance
When it comes to car insurance, there's a good chance that you might not be using the best place. Instead of being complacent and sticking with your current plan, consider shopping around to find a better one.

Principle #137 – Seek the Help of a Financial Advisor
When you first start to invest, seek out the help of a financial advisor. The successful know that it is not possible to know everything; and that getting the advice of a professional is always a good place to start.

Principle #138 – Shop Around for the Best Mortgage
Another thing that people who are successful in personal finance generally do is shop around for a mortgage. Instead of simply taking the first that they are offered at the first bank they go to, they test the waters with a number of different companies to try to get a lower interest rate.

In addition to shopping around with different banks, you may also want to shop around for different mortgage product types or visit a mortgage broker. Even if you ultimately do not use one of the companies or products they suggest, you can get a feel for what is out there in terms of payment sizes, interest rates, and other important features.

Principle #139 – Don't Buy a Big House if You Cannot Afford It
Locking yourself into a big mortgage payment is a very bad idea—especially if you have a shaky income. Instead of risking the possibility that might not be able to make the payments, settle for a smaller house or an apartment until you have financial capacity to make the payments on time. No matter where you live, there will most likely be taxes associated with homeownership. When switching from renting to a home, keep this in mind.

Principle #140 – Negotiate Selling Prices on Large Purchases
One stark distinction between the successful and the unsuccessful is that the successful are always willing to bargain. Even if it means that they'll have a much less pleasant buying experience, they'll spend hours haggling if it means they can cut hundreds or thousands off of the price tag.

Section #3: Success in Your Personal Life

No matter how well your work life is going, your personal life has the potential to drag everything down with it… or to enhance it.

If you're not happy and comfortable in your own home, then were can you be comfortable?

Below, we will consider how those who are successful in their relationships and personal lives behave and how you can change your behavior to become more like them.

Principle #141 – Dream Big and Turn Your Dreams into Action

One thing that the successful consistently do is dream big. But unlike most of us, they take those dreams and translate them into action—and, ultimately, positive outcomes. Success can mean different things to different people. Define what it means to you.

Does it mean that you become closer and more open with your spouse? Changing your financial situation? Being healthier? Once you define it, focus on achieving it. Without meaning, our lives are dull and depressing. With meaning, each day is full of memories and important milestones. So find ways to make your life meaningful, and if you are married or in a relationship, try to make it meaningful with your significant other.

Goals serve as a means for you to gauge your progress and to keep you focused on the future. So, do as the successful do, and set goals for your personal life. Take steps to achieve them. Remember, one step forward each day for a year gets you further than 50 steps forward gets you in a week. Everything cannot be accomplished overnight. Consistency and dedication will help you to see results over the long run.

Principle #142 – Reconcile with Family Members

If your personal life is riddled with conflicts, then you may want to take some time to step back and ask yourself what is going wrong.

You could try to be the bigger person and reconcile many conflicts with family members, rather than perpetuating them.

I spent most of my life estranged from the majority of my family. If it causes you lingering pain, try to work through it somehow. If you decide that distance is the answer, that is fine too.

Just remember, bitterness pulls from your positive energy in the world.

Unmanaged pain can stand in the way of success and joy.

Principle #143 – Set Relationship Goals

One thing that people who are successful in personal relationships do is set goals. For instance, they might consider the progression of a romantic relationship and consider whether it is going too quickly or too slowly. They might also try to look one year ahead and decide where they want to be, so they can steer the relationship in that direction.

From time to time, show your spouse the gratitude that he or she deserves. Don't hold back on praise or use it as a bargaining chip. Instead, be open honest, and loving; and you will receive the same in return.

Instead of seeing your spouse as a competitor, see him or her as a partner in life. Think about how you can work together to achieve better outcomes for both of you, rather than thinking about how you can get out of whatever task he or she wishes you to do.

No matter whether it is a romantic relationship or a friendship, strive for healthiness and transparency. Don't hide information. Don't do anything to intentionally hurt your friends or your partner. And, most of all, try to be honest and forthcoming in all of your endeavors.

Principle #144 – Develop Self-Confidence

While a little self-doubt usually isn't a bad thing, a lot of self-doubt can be highly destructive.

It can prevent you from accomplishing many things and it can prevent you from fully participating in relationships, as well as forming new relationships.

One of the mottos I live by is this: Competence breeds confidence.

Keep learning. Keep growing. Keep excelling. Confidence will come.

Principle #145 – Make an Effort to be Happy and Stay Disciplined

Make an effort to be happy at home and to spread that happiness to your spouse and children. No matter what challenges you face, try not to bring them home with you.

Successful people find ways to stay motivated and/or disciplined, no matter their circumstances.

You must also find something that keeps you fiery, dedicated, motivated, and hungry for more. Remember that motivation may come and go, but discipline will keep you steady when motivation is lacking.

Modeling your dedication to stay happy and continue moving forward toward achieving goals is often a very inspiring thing for your family to see, especially if you navigate this with poise and strength.

Principle #146 – Diet and Exercise is Important

Regardless of whatever else is going on in your life, proper diet and exercise is something successful people never stray too far from.

They know that a healthy body is an important supporting pillar of a healthy mind. A healthy diet helps people to maintain consistent energy levels.

Principle #147 – Let Go of Your Fear of Failure

On the road to success, you will experience many failures. This is why it is so important to let these fears go; and instead focus on the process of achieving those goals that you want so badly.

Principle #148 – Schedule Your Life

Instead of panicking about how disorganized events are in your life, make an effort to schedule things carefully. This will allow you to know what you need to do and when, rather than letting chance play the dominant role in determining your fate.

Principle #149 – Don't Let Your Past Limit Your Future

In the past, we have all failed miserably at many things.

That doesn't have to carry over into the future.

Don't let your past limit your future. Instead, let go of your past failures. Focus on what the future offers and how you can learn from failures instead of stay hung up on them.

Principle #150 – Remain Proactive in Tackling Challenges
Many of us go through life with unreasonably high expectations of what we can and should achieve. Over time, we readjust our expectations, but only after chasing something that ultimately ended up being a waste of time. Instead of doing this, do as the successful do and shoot high, but keep reasonable expectations.
If a big financial or personal event is looming on the horizon, be proactive in dealing with it. Set goals, and make an effort to break them down into manageable chunks. This will help you to stay positive and proactive in tackling the challenges ahead of you. Find ways to set and accomplish daily objectives that advance you further towards your goals. Little by little, you will get there.

Principle #151 – Take Notes
You're not in school anymore, but taking notes still has a lot of value. If you have ideas about how you can improve your personal or financial life, write them down too. Don't simply let these notes and insights slip away. Create lists with action items, and TAKE ACTION.

Principle #152 – Stop Blaming Others for Your Problem
While others may have the ability to make your problems worse, only you can solve them.
Stop blaming other people for your problems and take responsibility for your life and decisions.
Accountability with how we navigate challenges, avoid staying stuck, and charge forward to success will be critical for long term success in our personal lives.

Principle #153 – Spend Time Relaxing
From time to time, you should relax with your spouse and family. The successful know that hard work is important, but relaxation is equally important.

Principle #154 – Make Important Lifestyle Changes
In addition to improving your mindset, you should also consider making lifestyle changes where they are warranted. For instance, you may want to cut down on excessive drinking or you may want to stop smoking. Take some time to evaluate your life and lifestyle. Consider where you have come from and where you are likely to end up. Decide whether you want to deviate from this path to achieve a better outcome. Then, implement your plan to create change.

Principle #155 – Try to Do Good Things Each Day
Each day, try to do something good for other people. Help a co-worker.
Contribute to a charity. Help your spouse with something he or she is dreading. Whatever you do, make an effort to do something that no only helps someone else, but makes you feel better, too.
I know you've probably heard, "Give and you shall receive."
I don't think many of us have ever heard, "Receive. Then give. Then, you shall receive again."
Try to stay thoughtful and generous, without being careless or risking your well being.

I have a great deal of trust that good things will come my way, if I continue to work hard for them.

Conclusion

Finally, one of the most important things that successful people do is make sure they are at peace with the world and their own life. Even if their work life is riddled with conflict and controversy, they find a way to become comfortable with it all, so that it does not drag them down each day.

I hope that these tips have been helpful for you, because these tips have helped me find success throughout my life. They have allowed me to find peace with the world and to navigate challenges with a positive mindset.

I often find it helpful to reflect back on them from time to time or to pick one, set daily goals around it, and focus on making it a priority for a period of time. I journal about how I have succeeded in implementing this tip, so it forces me to keep my actions are the forefront of my mind.

It doesn't matter whether you are trying to improve your role in your business, in the workplace, or at home, there are people out there who have experienced success in these domains because they approach things with a strong mind and with goal-oriented approaches.

So get out there, and start working! You know what drives success. It's just a matter of adopting the applicable tips and making them work for you.

I wish you the best!

Epilogue

Did you like this book?
Then you'll LOVE our other business development resources.
Click here now to get:
Customizable Digital Wealth Builder Course
Custom Templates on Canva You Can Use to Create Digital Products
Monat Partnership Information for Hair & Beauty Sales Business Opportunity
Website Hosting
Accounting Software
Online Store Creation Software
Our Custom Sales Funnel

Please know that our company is an affiliate marketing company and may receive a commission for certain sales made through links on shared websites. These commissions would come at no additional cost to you. We are also network marketing partners and support building connections with specific brands, to help create streams of revenue for ourselves and our clients. No results can be guaranteed.

www.ingramcontent.com/pod-product-compliance
Lightning Source LLC
Chambersburg PA
CBHW070956220526
45471CB00007B/3050